It's all about…

SLITHERING
SNAKES

KINGFISHER

KINGFISHER

First published 2017 by Kingfisher
an imprint of Macmillan Children's Books
20 New Wharf Road, London N1 9RR
Associated companies throughout the world
www.panmacmillan.com

Series editor: Sarah Snashall
Design: WildPixel Ltd
Written by: Sarah Snashall

ISBN 978-0-7534-4151-0

Copyright © Macmillan Publishers International Ltd 2017

9 8 7 6 5 4 3 2 1

1TR/0717/WKT/UG/128MA

A CIP catalogue record for this book is available from the British Library.

Printed in China

Picture credits
The Publisher would like to thank the following for permission to reproduce their material.
Top = t; Bottom = b; Centre = c; Left = l; Right = r
Cover: Shutterstock/Will. E. Davis; Back cover: iStock/GlobalP; Pages: 2-3, 30-31 iStock/
FroeMic; 4 iStock/artush; 5 Blair Hedges, Penn State; 6 iStock/yotrak, 7 Getty/Thierry
Montford; 7b iStock/draskovic; 8 iStock/gowrivaranashi; 9 iStock/Mark Kostich; 10-11 Alamy/
Roger Clark; 11 Alamy/Aterra Picture Library; 12 Alamy/Nick Greaves; 13 iStock/JedsPics_
com; 13t iStock/reptiles4all; 14 iStock/Dragisa; 15t Getty/Morales; 15b Shutterstock/Heiko
Kiera; 16 iStock/thawats; 17t Shutterstock/Business Stock; 17b iStock/Snowleopard1;
18-19 Alamy/scubazoo; 19 Shutterstock/Vadim Petrakov; 20 iStock/lensomy; 21 Shutterstock/
Stuart G Porter; 22 iStock/sergeyskieznev; 23 Shutterstock/Natalia kuzmina; 24-25 Getty;
24b iStock/bgwalker; 25 Alamy/Nature Picture Library; 26 iStock/Byronsdad; 27t iStock/
JenniferPhotograhyImaging; 28 iStock/sergeyryzhov; 29t iStock/RapidEye; 29b iStock/
EdwardDerule
Cards: front tl SPL/Jaime Chirinos; tr iStock/Mark Kostich; bl iStock/emmgunn; br iStock
Markcurclo; back tl iStock/singularone; tr iStock/shannonplummer; bl Shutterstock/Gerald A
DeBouer; br iStock/Mark Kostich.

Front cover: A bush viper lies in wait for its prey.

CONTENTS

What is a snake?   4

A snake's body   6

Scaly skin   8

Moving along   10

Dinner time   12

Eggs and babies   14

Biter or squeezer?   16

Life in the water   18

Cobras   20

A deadly squeeze   22

Rattlers   24

Snakes in danger   26

Snakes as pets   28

Glossary   30

Index   32

What is a snake?

Snakes are a type of reptile. They are cold-blooded, which means their body temperature matches that of their environment. There are over 3400 types of snake and all are meat-eaters and skilled hunters.

FACT...

Snakes can be found on every continent, except Antarctica, but there are no snakes in Iceland, Ireland and New Zealand.

Longest snake: reticulated python – up to 8 metres
Fastest snake: black mamba – 19 kilometres an hour
Smallest snake: Barbados threadsnake – 10 centimetres
Heaviest snake: green anaconda – 1100 kilograms or more
Most dangerous snake: saw-scaled viper
Most toxic snake: inland taipan

This vine snake uses its forked tongue to 'smell' prey.

Barbados threadsnake

A snake's body

A snake's throat makes up one third of its body! All its other organs, such as stomach, liver, kidneys and gut, are long and thin and stacked one after the other down its body.

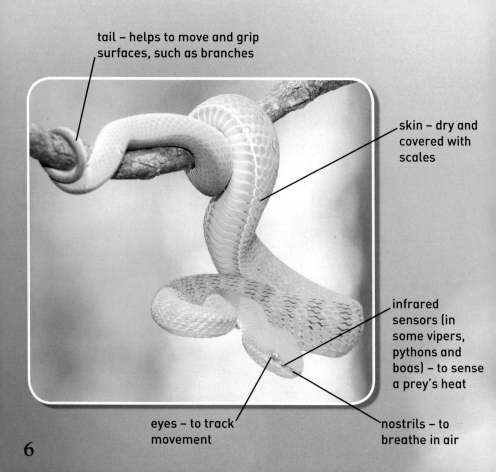

tail – helps to move and grip surfaces, such as branches

skin – dry and covered with scales

infrared sensors (in some vipers, pythons and boas) – to sense a prey's heat

eyes – to track movement

nostrils – to breathe in air

A snake can have as many as 400 vertebrae. Humans only have about 33 vertebrae.

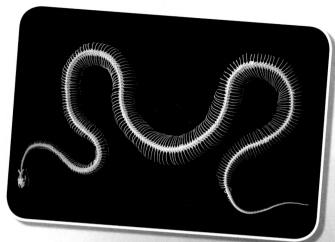

teeth – hollow fangs inject venom

jaws – separate to stretch wide

Scaly skin

A snake's skin is made up of thousands of tiny scales of keratin (the same material as human nails). The scales make a surface that is smooth in one direction and rough in the other – this helps the snake to move and to grip trees.

A snake's scales lie flat on top of each other.

Every few months, a snake sheds the top dead layer of skin. It rubs a hole in the skin near its mouth and crawls out, turning the skin inside out on the way.

This snake is shedding its skin.

The venomous spiny bush viper has colourful, spiky scales.

SPOTLIGHT: Spiny bush viper

Fact:	ambushes prey in trees
Maximum length:	73 centimetres
Habitat:	rainforests in central Africa
Diet:	rodents, birds, lizards, frogs

Moving along

Snakes move amazingly fast although they have no arms or legs.

A sidewinder snake keeps much of its body off the hot sand as it moves.

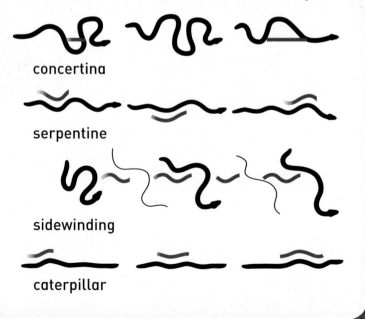

Snakes move in one of four different ways.

concertina

serpentine

sidewinding

caterpillar

Most snakes grip the ground with the rough scales on their belly and push away from this using their muscles – a bit like a runner with grippy trainers. This is called serpentine movement.

In water, snakes move their tail from side to side to move forwards.

Dinner time

A snake's throat and neck can expand
to eat incredible-sized meals. Its jaws
and ribs separate and stretch wide.
It can take days, or even weeks, for
a snake to digest its meal.

Snakes swallow their prey whole.

FACT...

In 2005 a python exploded when
it tried to eat an alligator.

To prevent choking as it swallows, a snake will push its windpipe out of its mouth like a snorkel.

Rear-facing teeth stop prey from escaping.

Large snakes that eat huge prey only need to eat every few months.

Eggs and babies

Most snakes lay eggs, usually leaving them in a warm, safe place. Where the climate is too cool for eggs to develop, snakes gives birth to live babies.

FACT...

African rock pythons are the only snakes that stay to protect their young.

Baby snakes are immediately able to fend for themselves.

Some snakes will wrap their body
around their eggs to keep them warm.

Baby snakes use an 'egg tooth' to
break out of their leathery shell.

Biter or squeezer?

Snakes are the most efficient killers. Most snakes, such as vipers and cobras, are biters, injecting venom through their hollow fangs.

Every time the prey breathes out, the constrictor tightens its deadly squeeze.

Some snakes, such as boas and pythons, squeeze their prey until it stops breathing – then they swallow it whole!

Some snakes are 'milked' for their venom to make anti-venom.

FACT...

The eyelash viper will wait at the same ambush site each year to catch migrating birds.

SPOTLIGHT: Eyelash viper

Fact:	spiky scales above eyes
Maximum length:	about 80 centimetres
Habitat:	Central and South America
Diet:	rodents, frogs, birds

Life in the water

All snakes can swim but some spend most of their time in the water, only coming to the surface to breathe.

Living in the warm Indian Ocean, the banded sea krait has a tail like a paddle and can stay underwater for an hour without breathing.

Fact:	heaviest snake in the world
Maximum length:	8.8 metres
Habitat:	South American swamps, rivers
Diet:	fish, birds, tapirs, capybaras

The banded sea krait eats moray eels.

Cobras

Cobras are venomous snakes found
in hot areas of Africa and
Asia. When threatened,
a cobra raises its body
to a standing position,
hisses and spreads its
neck ribs to create
an awesome hood.

A cobra can lift up
a third of its body.

The spitting cobra spits venom into the eyes of a would-be attacker.

FACT...

The king cobra can inject enough venom to kill an elephant!

SPOTLIGHT: King cobra

Fact:	only snake to make a nest
Maximum length:	5.5 metres
Habitat:	Indian and Asian rainforests
Diet:	snakes, birds, mammals

A deadly squeeze

Pythons and boas are monster snakes that kill by constriction. They live in hot countries where their huge body can stay warm.

The green tree python places its head in the middle of its body to rest.

These snakes have heat sensors to help them track warm-blooded animals in the dark. The massive reticulated python is the world's longest snake.

Younger and smaller boa constrictors often live in trees.

FACT...

In South America people keep boa constrictors as pets to kill rats.

Rattlers

Rattlesnakes are a type of pit viper found in North America, Central America and South America. They have rings of dead skin on their tail, which they rattle to warn predators to stay away.

CAUTION

THERE MAY BE
RATTLESNAKES IN THIS AREA.

FACT...

Each time a rattlesnake sheds its skin, it adds a new ring to its rattle.

The rings of the rattle knock together to make the rattle sound.

The large and dangerous Eastern diamondback rattlesnake has long fangs.

Snakes in danger

Most snakes in the wild are not endangered. However, the habitat of many types of snake is disappearing due to farming and growing cities.

Some snakes are killed for their skin. Millions of pounds' worth of fashion goods are made with illegal snake skin every year.

Pythons are most commonly killed to make bags and shoes from their skin.

The critically endangered golden lancehead only exists on a small island in Brazil.

Snakes as pets

Many snakes can make good pets if they are properly looked after. Surprisingly even large snakes such as pythons can make easy pets, as they are not aggressive.

Brave (and careful) people also manage to keep venomous snakes safely.

Some people like the excitement of owning a dangerous snake.

FACT...

Snakes cannot actually hear the music of a snake charmer. They respond to the movement of the flute.

A snake charmer pretends to hypnotize cobras.

GLOSSARY

ambush To attack suddenly, often from a hidden place.

Antarctica The area around the South Pole.

anti-venom A medicine used to treat people who have been bitten by a venomous snake.

constriction The act of squeezing tighter and tighter.

digest To use chemicals in the stomach to break down food into substances that the body can use.

endangered In danger of dying out.

fang A long, pointed and sometimes hollow tooth through which a snake injects venom into its prey.

fend To look after or find food for.

habitat The type of place where an animal lives. Deserts and forests are two different habitats.

hypnotize To send into a kind of sleep-like state.

illegal Against the law.

organ A part of the body that does a specific job, such as the heart.

prey An animal that another animal hunts for food.

reptile A type of cold-blooded animal that normally lays eggs and has scaly skin. Crocodiles, turtles and snakes are reptiles.

reticulated Like a net. For snakes this means having a complex pattern on their skin.

serpentine Like a snake.

toxic Poisonous.

venom A poison made by snakes, spiders and scorpions. It is usually injected through fangs, or a stinger, into a victim.

vertebrae Bones that link together to form the backbone, or spine, of an animal.

windpipe The tube that takes air from the mouth to the lungs.

INDEX

African rock pythons 14

anacondas, green 5, 18

anti-venom 17

babies 14–15

banded sea kraits 19

Barbados threadsnakes
  5

black mambas 5

boas 22–23

bodies 6–7, 10–11,
  12–13, 22–23

cobras 16, 20–21, 29

constrictors 16, 22–23

Eastern diamond back
  rattlesnakes 25

eating 9, 12–13, 16, 17,
  18, 21

egg tooth 15

eggs 14–15

eyelash vipers 17

fangs 7, 16, 25

habitats 4, 9, 14, 17, 18,
  20–21, 24, 26

king cobras 21

movement 8, 10–11

pets 23, 28–29

pythons 5, 12, 14,
  22–23, 28

rattlesnakes 24–25

reticulated pythons 5

saw-scaled vipers 5

scales see skin

sidewinder snakes 10–11

skin 7, 8–9, 11, 17, 27

snake charmers 29

spiny bush vipers 9

spitting cobras 21

taipans 5

teeth 7, 13

venom 16, 17, 29

vine snakes 4

vipers 5, 9, 16, 17, 24–25

water snakes 11, 18–19

Collect all the titles in this series!

BEASTLY BUGS

FREE Collector Cards and Downloadable Audio!

DEADLY DINOSAURS

FREE Collector Cards and Downloadable Audio!

EPIC EXPLORERS

FREE Collector Cards and Downloadable Audio!

EXOTIC EGYPTIANS

FREE Collector Cards and Downloadable Audio!

FANTASTIC FLIERS

FREE Collector Cards and Downloadable Audio!

FAST CARS

FREE Collector Cards and Downloadable Audio!

FREEZING POLES

FREE Collector Cards and Downloadable Audio!

GLORIOUS GREEKS

FREE Collector Cards and Downloadable Audio!

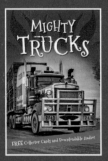

MIGHTY TRUCKS

FREE Collector Cards and Downloadable Audio!

REMARKABLE ROMANS

FREE Collector Cards and Downloadable Audio!

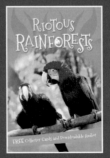

RIOTOUS RAINFORESTS

FREE Collector Cards and Downloadable Audio!

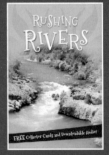

RUSHING RIVERS

FREE Collector Cards and Downloadable Audio!